Rabén & Sjögren Stockholm

Library of Congress catalog card number: 87-15016
Originally published in Sweden under the title
Linnea planterar; kärnor, frön och annat by Rabén & Sjögren, 1978
First American edition 1988
Fourth printing 1992
Printed in Italy

R & S Books are distributed in the United States of America
by Farrar, Straus and Giroux, New York;
in the United Kingdom by Ragged Bears Andover;
in Canada by General Publishing, Toronto;
and in Australia by ERA Publications, Adelaide.

ISBN 91 29 59064 7

Linnea's Windowsill Garden

By Christina Björk and Lena Anderson

Translated by Joan Sandin

R&S BOOKS

Stockholm New York London Adelaide

Thank you

Björn Berglund, who checked our facts;
Stig Sandell, who runs a plant nursery
and has answered our endless questions;
and Nicolina Anderson, thirteen years
old, who has helped us with planting
and watering ever since she was eight years old.

CONTENTS

_Hi!_

My name is Linnea

I like flowers, and leaves and stems and seeds — in fact I like everything that grows. I even like my name. I am named after the linnaea, a little pink flower that grows in the woods.

CAROLUS LINNAEUS WITH A LINNAEA IN HIS BUTTONHOLE

The flower linnaea is named after Carolus Linnaeus. He liked flowers, too. He studied all the ones he could collect and wrote about them in a large book. He also gave the flowers their Latin names.

The linnaea was Linnaeus's favorite flower. That's why he named it after himself. Its last name is Boreális, which means northern.

I'm no woodland flower (even if my name is Linnea). I'm an asphalt flower. I live in the city, where there are no forests or fields, but I am surrounded with green things anyway. All over my apartment — in flowerpots and boxes and cans, things are growing!

THIS IS
WHAT A LINNEA LOOKS LIKE,
THIS SWEDISH STAMP
WAS ISSUED IN 1978,
TWO HUNDRED YEARS AFTER
LINNAEUS'S DEATH

SVERIGE 130

I have a good friend whose name is Mr. Bloom (not a bad name for someone who is a retired gardener).

"Why do your plants always look so healthy?" I ask him.

"I guess I just have a green thumb," says Mr. Bloom.

"A GREEN THUMB! Your thumb isn't green!" (Maybe a little brown, I think, because of all that digging around in the dirt.)

"It is green," says Mr. Bloom. "You just can't see it. Only my plants can. You see, having a 'green thumb' means having a talent for raising plants."

"Oh, then I want to have a green thumb, too!" I tell him.

"You'll get one," he says, "if you work with plants. In fact, I think you might already have a pale-green thumb. I can see that from your orange tree."

Oh, yes, my orange tree! Let me tell you about it.

↑ ME

MR. BLOOM ↑

Look at my orange tree!

In late December I planted some orange seeds, and now I have a real little orange tree. Here's what I did:

I bought some compressed peat pellets at a plant nursery and poured water on one of them. It started to swell up right away. A little more water and it was two inches high. Then I stuck in some orange seeds, poking them down into the peat with a pencil. I wrote ORANGE and the date on a little toothpick sign. Then I waited. And I watered the peat so it wouldn't dry out.

Only one of the seeds germinated (started to grow). After a couple of months, it

PEAT PELLET AND WATER

SEEDS

had become a little tree. (Orange seeds grow faster in the spring, from February on.)

When the tree was about three inches high, I replanted it in a flowerpot.

I put a potsherd (a piece of a broken clay pot) in the bottom, over the draining hole. Then I filled the pot with potting soil and watered it until it felt moist. Now I was ready to plant my orange tree, peat pellet and all. After it was in place, I added more soil, pressing down firmly (but not TOO firmly) around both the stem and the peat pellet.

Of course, you can also plant the seeds directly in the soil if you don't have a peat pellet.

HERE'S HOW IT GROWS BEST

An orange tree likes light, especially sunlight (as long as it's not too hot). Extra light from a lamp is good, too (see page 56). So is warm air from a radiator. But then you'll need to water more often. During the winter, an orange tree likes to be in a cool place.

Spray the leaves often with water.

An orange tree wants to be fed (fertilized) in the spring, summer, and fall.

If you're lucky, your tree will bloom after three years but mine never has).

9

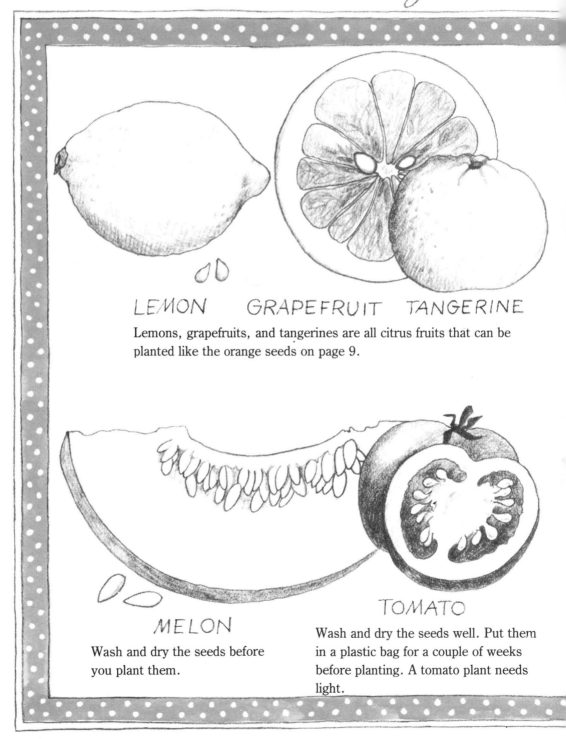

LEMON GRAPEFRUIT TANGERINE

Lemons, grapefruits, and tangerines are all citrus fruits that can be planted like the orange seeds on page 9.

MELON

Wash and dry the seeds before you plant them.

TOMATO

Wash and dry the seeds well. Put them in a plastic bag for a couple of weeks before planting. A tomato plant needs light.

MOST PITS CAN BE PLANTED LIKE ORANGE SEEDS.

can plant

BELL PEPPER

Dry the seeds for a few days. Put the pot in a light, warm place.

GRAPES

Dry and plant several seeds in the same pot.

AVOCADO

This one is really fun! Read about it on the next page.

YOU CAN READ ABOUT PITS THAT TAKE LONGER ON PAGE 56.

Avocado, my favorite

The best thing about an avocado plant is that it gets so big. It can grow to three feet or more. But mine hasn't gotten quite that tall yet.

HERE'S WHAT YOU DO

Take the pit from a RIPE avocado. Wash it in warm water and let it dry for twenty-four hours. It's best if the brown skin on the outside cracks.

Plant the pit (point up) in moist soil, so that a third of it remains aboveground. Put a plastic bag with air holes over the pot. That way, the air inside will stay moist and you won't have to water so often. It's important that the soil not dry out.

Now you have to wait. It can take three weeks or three months — you never know.

Oh, look! There it comes! Now you can fill the pot with soil, covering the whole pit.

An avocado plant wants light, but it dries out easily. Water it often, but not too

AVOCADO 2/23

AVOCADO 2/23

UGH, ONLY AN UGLY STICK LEFT...

4/24

5/24

pit

TIME TO PRUNE!

much. And spray the leaves with water every day.

When an avocado has gotten about nine inches high, it's time to prune. It feels terrible to cut off all the pretty new leaves and have nothing but a poor old stick left.

But if you don't prune your plant, you'll have nothing but one long skinny stem.

Look! Two new branches are growing where I cut off the stem, and both of them have new leaves. When they've grown a bit more, the new branches will also need to be pruned, and the ones that come after them, and so on.

Since leaves make a plant's food (see page 33), it's strange that an avocado plant can survive without a single leaf. Not all plants can do that, so ask for advice before pruning other plants.

AVOCADO
2/23

. . . BUT AFTER
ONLY SEVEN WEEKS
IT LOOKED
THIS NICE!

7/15

Scarlet, the fastest bean in town

ACTUAL SIZE

Sometimes I get so tired of waiting for lazy old seeds that take forever to grow! That's why I bought a packet of scarlet runner beans (from the phaseolus family).

I named one of the beans Scarlet and planted her about an inch deep in a small flowerpot (not too small).

Then I watered the soil until it felt moist, and put the pot near the radiator.

That was on April 10.

Already, on the fourteenth, some small green leaves were poking up out of the soil! After that, Scarlet grew furiously, more than an inch a day.

I had to put a stick in the pot for her to climb on.

AFTER TWO WEEKS, SCARLET WAS AS TALL AS ME!

I took down my curtain and stretched a string from the bottom of the window frame up to the curtain rod. Then, very carefully, I showed Scarlet how to climb the string.

After that, I planted four more beans. They are just coming up now — except one (and it looks as if that one isn't going to come up at all).

P.S. After a while, Scarlet and the other scarlet runners grew beautiful red flowers. If you move the plants outside (to a balcony or garden), they will produce GIANT pods. Inside each pod you'll find the very same kind of bean you started out with. Isn't THAT amazing!

WARNING!

Both the pods and the beans are POISON-OUS, but you can eat them if you cook them first.

PS. DON'T BE DISAPPOINTED WHEN YOUR SCARLET RUNNER BEAN DIES.
IT'S ONLY AN ANNUAL. NEXT SPRING, YOU CAN PLANT ANOTHER ONE

Why did Scarlet start to grow when I planted her, and not when she was still in the seed packet? I'd better ask Mr. Bloom.

"It takes three things to make a seed start to grow," says Mr. Bloom. "Water, oxygen, and heat. It was cool and dry in the seed packet, but when you put Scarlet in the warm, moist soil, she started sucking up water. With the help of the water and oxygen in the soil, Scarlet could start growing.

"She grew above and below the soil. Above, she grew leaves, and below, she grew roots. She needed both in order to get the necessary nourishment."

"But how could she be alive BEFORE she got any food?" I ask.

"She had her lunchbox with her," says Mr. Bloom. "A bean is made up of a shell with seed protein inside. The protein is the 'lunchbox' that kept Scarlet alive until she got her roots and leaves.

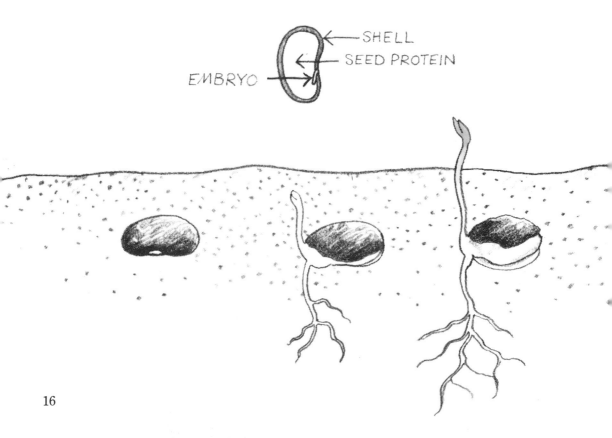

EMBRYO

SHELL
SEED PROTEIN

to grow?

HOW DOES SCARLET KNOW WHICH END IS UP?

"Inside the seed protein is the embryo itself, alive and WAITING — waiting for the water and heat that will make it grow."

"But what makes it ALIVE?" I ask, because I want to know EVERYTHING.

"THAT I don't know," says Mr. Bloom. "Those are the hardest questions of all, you know — questions about LIFE ITSELF."

"What if Scarlet had grown all wrong?" I ask. "What if she had grown sideways instead of upwards?"

"Scarlet knows which direction is up, just as you do. The force of gravity makes her want to grow UP. And her roots want to grow DOWN to get nourishment from the soil."

"What would have happened if Scarlet's pot had tipped over?" I ask.

"Then she would have changed directions," says Mr. Bloom, "and continued growing upwards until she ran into the side of the pot."

"And what if we turned the pot upright again? Would she turn and grow up through the soil?"

"That's just what she would do," says Mr. Bloom.

GET READY FOR THE PEA OLYMPICS! TURN THE PAGE!

17

It's fun to SEE how something grows. Peas, beans, and lentils are the most fun to watch, because they sprout and grow so quickly. First, we'll feature a contest of strength:

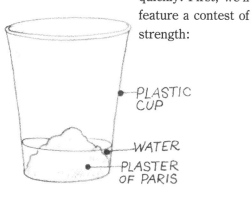

- PLASTIC CUP
- WATER
- PLASTER OF PARIS

Put some water in a plastic cup. Pour in some plaster of Paris (not the other way around), until small plaster "islands" start to form.

- CANDY MOLD

Stir and quickly pour the plaster into molds. Bury a pea in each one. When the plaster hardens, remove the mold.

WARNING: DON'T POUR PLASTER INTO THE SINK! IT CLOGS THE DRAIN!

WHO IS STRONGEST?

COME ON, KARL!

Here are Vera, Albert, and Karl (the three split peas I buried in plaster). They are sucking up the water from the plaster and starting to sprout. When they sprout, they swell up and break their way out of the plaster. That's what I call Pea Power!

THE RESULT

Vera won! She broke out after two hours. Karl came out after three, and Albert didn't come out at all.

WHO WILL SPROUT FIRST?

I placed the four contestants in a glass jar, lined on the bottom with wet cotton. They were:

Split Pea Pete
Green Pea Polly
Lentil Larry
and Scarlet Runner-Bean Rosalyn.
The race started on April 19.

WHO WILL GROW FASTEST?

This contest was only for split peas: Ernie, Arnold, and Nicky. I poked each one down in its own peat pellet (look at page 9 to see how to do it). When they came up, I gave them each a stick to climb on.

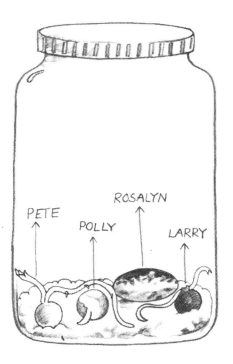

THE RESULT

Pete won. After five days (on April 24), this is how the inside of the jar looked. Rosalyn still hadn't sprouted. (Not all scarlet runner beans are as energetic as Scarlet!)

THE RESULT

Arnold won, hands down. Ernie came in second, and Nicky wilted. (Maybe I didn't give her enough water and her peat pellet dried out.)

Now I'll tell you about my nicest plant. Her name is Busy Lizzie. That's a good name for her because Lizzie definitely is busy: she never stops growing and blooming. This is how I got my first Busy Lizzie:

Mr. Bloom had a large plant and he let me take a cutting from it. That means cutting off a little branch, so that it can later take root and grow up to be a new plant.

HERE'S HOW YOU MAKE A CUTTING

Usually, you take a cutting from the top of the "parent plant," but you can also take a side cutting.

Cut off the shoot with a sharp knife (don't break it off) just ABOVE one of the leaves. A new little shoot will be able to

grow out at the leaf node of the "parent plant."

I picked a shoot that had four leaves and no flowers or buds. (It would be too hard for a small shoot to support flowers when it's just starting out on its own.)

Then I took the cutting home in a plastic bag. Just before putting it in a glass of water, I cut it once more (with a sharp knife), UNDER the lowest leaf. It's right there, at the leaf node, that a plant is most likely to put out new roots. Then I cut off the lowest leaf, so the cutting could stand up better in the glass.

Next I put a plastic bag (with air holes) over both the glass and the cutting. That was to keep water from evaporating off the leaves.

Don't worry if your cutting starts to droop in the beginning. It has suffered a shock, being cut off from its "parent."

After a week, small roots started growing from my cutting. And after two weeks they were almost an inch long.

3

TIME FOR PLANTING!

I take out a good-sized flowerpot for my Busy Lizzie, since she will be growing fast. (You can read all about flowerpots on page 51.) I put a piece of broken pottery over the hole in the bottom of the pot. That way, the water can drain but the soil won't fall out.

4

Then I fill the pot with soil, but no higher than two inches from the top. I water it until it starts to drip out the hole. Then I know the soil is moist all the way through.

Now I put my little Lizzie in the pot and fill it with soil, pressing down firmly (but not TOO firmly). The soil still shouldn't be all the way up to the top, or there will be no place to water the plant.

I leave the plastic bag over both the plant and the pot the first five days, until the roots have gotten used to their new home.

Then, I just watch her grow. Turn the page and you'll see what I mean.

In no time at all, my little Lizzie had become a big Lizzie. Actually, it's wrong to call Mr. Bloom's Lizzie the parent and mine the child, since they are really the SAME plant, or the same INDIVIDUAL, as Mr. Bloom would say. A new individual can only come from a new seed. (You can read more about that on page 40.)

IMPATIENS WALLERIANA

That's the Latin name for Busy Lizzie. She belongs to the balsam family (Balsaminaceae). "Sultan's balsam" is another one of Lizzie's many names.

Lizzie's ancestors live in the tropical forests of East Africa and on the island of Zanzibar. There they grow wild.

Busy Lizzie blooms nearly all year round, except for the darkest weeks in December.

Her flowers are bright red, red-orange, pink, salmon, white, or purple. I think I like the pink ones best.

LIZZIE LIKES

HEAT

Lizzie doesn't want to be cold. She likes it to be about 70°F. in the winter. If her leaves fall off and she doesn't get any buds, it's probably because she's too cold.

WATER

The warmer and lighter it is, the more water Lizzie will need. But don't water too much, or her stem will rot! Don't spray a Busy Lizzie when she's blooming, either (and she's nearly always blooming).

FERTILIZER

Lizzie will need some plant food (fertilizer) in her water, once a week, from March to September.

WARNING!

Lizzie gets bugs easily, so check her every now and then. If she has mites, she is getting too much summer sun. If the air is too dry, she can get aphids or whiteflies. (You can learn how to get rid of bugs on page 44.)

my big Lizzie!

Now I'm going to tell you everything I know about watering plants, since it's VERY important to know, if you want your plants to survive.

MORE PLANTS DIE OF TOO <u>MUCH</u> WATER

THAN OF TOO LITTLE WATER!

Both the leaves and the roots of a plant need air to breathe and stay alive. If you water too much, the air can't push its way down through the soaking-wet soil and reach the roots. They will suffocate and the plant will eventually die.

That's why you should water only when it's needed.

BUT HOW CAN YOU TELL WHEN A PLANT NEEDS WATER?

Before watering your plant, check the soil. If it feels cold and moist, then it doesn't need water. If it feels dry, water it.

You can also knock on the pot. If you hear a "CLONK," the soil inside is dry (and has pulled away from the sides of the pot). Water immediately! If you hear a "CLINK," the soil is probably moist.

WATER DEEPLY!

The worst thing you can do is to be stingy when you water your plants, so that the water can't reach down to the roots. (In the worst cases, the roots can even start growing UP in order to get to the water!) Deep-water your plants, so that the soil is wet all

watering

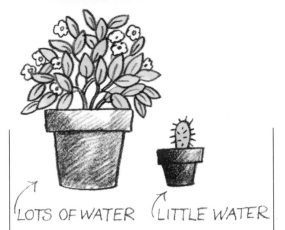

the way through. The excess water can run out into a draining dish under the pot.

I usually water my plants (the ones that need it, that is) before I eat breakfast. Then, when I'm finished eating, I go around and empty all the draining dishes.

LOTS OF WATER   LITTLE WATER

All plants need more water when they're growing and less when they're resting. And they will dry out faster in the summer (when it's hot) than in the winter.

Plants do NOT like standing with their feet (I mean their roots) in water. I'm sure you can understand why.

If I didn't empty out the excess water, the roots and soil could start to rot. Or start to crawl with small white worms. Yuck!

NOT ALL PLANTS NEED THE SAME AMOUNT OF WATER

Large leafy plants and plants in big pots need more water than small plants in little pots. And desert plants, like cacti, need less water than tropical rain-forest plants like ferns.

HELP!
I FORGOT TO WATER MY
BUSY LIZZIE!

One day I noticed that one of my Busy Lizzies was drooping. Her soil was like a dry lump in the pot. I had forgotten to water her! What should I do?

WATER UP OVER THE TOP OF THE POT

I quickly filled a big bowl with water and put Lizzie in it, with the water level up over the top of her pot. I left her like that for quite a while, until no more bubbles came to the surface.

And, believe it or not, after a couple of hours she began to recover and to stand up straight. Lizzie was saved!

25

RECIPE FOR PLANT WATER

Plants don't like water right out of the tap. It's too cold, and it contains too much chlorine and often too much calcium. Water that is high in calcium is called "hard water." Rainwater, on the other hand, is "soft water," and plants love it — except here in the city, where rainwater is so contaminated by engine exhaust and industrial pollution that it is more likely to be harmful to plants.

That's why I make my own plant water:

I fill a watering can and several bottles with tap water (we use lots of water at my house these days). Then I let them stand near the radiator overnight. By morning, the chlorine has evaporated and the calcium has sunk to the bottom. The water is just the right temperature, too, and plants like THAT. They don't want an ice-cold shower in the morning any more than you do!

So that I don't forget, I always refill my watering can as soon as I've watered my plants in the morning. That way, everything is ready to go the next day.

A WATERING CAN

is good to have. It should have a spout long enough to reach all the places you'll need to water.

If you don't have a watering can, you can use an ordinary bottle instead.

SHOWER EVERY DAY!

Get yourself a spray bottle (mister) and give your plants a daily shower. They'll love it, since the air in heated rooms is almost always too dry for them.

The only time you should NOT spray a plant is when it is blooming. Busy Lizzie, for example, does not want to get her flowers wet — they can get ugly spots on them.

A SPRAY BOTTLE

costs a little money, but it can be used for other things around the house (like sprinkling the ironing). So maybe you won't have to pay for one with your allowance . . .

When you go away

There are lots of tricks for watering plants when you're not at home. Here are a few that I use:

WATERING WITH A STRING

In stores that sell plants and seeds, you can buy cheap plastic-covered watering wicks. Fill a large container with water and stick one end of a watering wick in it, all the way to the bottom. Push the other end down into your plant's soil.

Water from the container will be drawn up through the wick and over to the plant.

(I've heard that wool or cotton yarn works as well, but don't use synthetic yarn.)

Try it while you're home and see how long the water holds out (it depends a little on how warm it is). Then you'll know just how long you can be away before you have to ask a neighbor to water your plants.

ANOTHER TRICK

Cut out a strip of cloth and stuff it up the hole in the bottom of the pot. Put the pot over a jar of water, with the strip hanging down into the water.

A THIRD TRICK

Put several layers of wet newspaper in the bathtub, and set the pots on that. Strangely enough, the plants will be able to survive for several weeks. There should be a window in the bathroom, though, so the plants can get the light they need to make their food.

IMPORTANT: This trick does NOT work with plants that need LOTS of water (like Busy Lizzie), but it's fine for cacti, palms, and rubber plants.

The water cycle

"I just water and water and water," I say to Mr. Bloom. "What do my plants do with all that water? It can't just disappear, can it?"

"No, it doesn't disappear," says Mr. Bloom. "I'd better tell you about Mother Nature's water cycle.

"When water dries up," Mr. Bloom explains, "it mixes with air, and we say that it EVAPORATES and becomes water vapor.

"Water is evaporating everywhere — from lakes and oceans, from the ground, from the soil in your flowerpots, and from the plants themselves. When the plants

don't need the water that they've sucked up anymore, they release it into the air through their leaves.

"When you breathe, you release water vapor, too. Try breathing on a windowpane and you'll see. The mist is made up of tiny drops of water."

7. THEIR LEAVES "BREATHE" OUT THE WATER WHICH EVAPORATES

8. NEW CLOUDS FORM, ETC.

5. PLANTS AND TREES SUCK UP THE RAINWATER

THE SUN DRIVES THE WATER CYCLE

"When the sun warms up the earth's surface, the warm air near the earth rises. The water vapor in the air follows it, and when it's risen high enough, clouds are formed.

"The clouds continue to climb, and when they cool down, it starts to rain. The water has returned. Everything that is growing where the rain falls starts sucking up the water with its roots and stems.

"Then the water is carried out to the leaves and 'breathed' out once more. It evaporates. The sun warms up the air again and it rises."

"Stop right there!" I tell him. "Or we'll be going around another time!"

MY OWN LITTLE WATER CYCLE

"That's how Mother Nature's BIG water cycle works," says Mr. Bloom. "But you can make your own LITTLE water cycle."

"Really?" I ask. "Well, then, let's do it right now!"

First, we found a large glass jar (it must be at least three-quart size).

It's important that the jar is perfectly clean and dry.

We lined the bottom of the jar with charcoal (to prevent mold), and over that, we put a layer of sterile potting soil. (You can buy both where plants are sold.) Together they should fill a quarter of the jar.

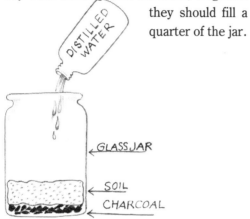

We made a little hole in the middle of the soil and planted a peperomia that Mr. Bloom had given me. You should choose a plant that grows SLOWLY, so it won't outgrow the jar right away.

Then I put in George and Martha (two small china rabbits) and a plastic angel.

(A pig made of clay was NOT a good idea. It got moldy, and mold is a plant jar's worst enemy. Glass, china, and plastic are the only materials that work.)

NO TAP WATER!!!

Then we carefully poured in DISTILLED water. Ordinary tap water isn't pure enough.

(Distilled water is what you use in steam irons and car batteries. You can buy it at gas stations and drugstores.)

If you're using a three-quart jar, you will need only a half cup of water. That doesn't sound like much, but it's enough!

Finally we covered the jar with plastic wrap, held in place with a rubber band.

After that, we didn't open it anymore. And we didn't water it, either! The jar needs light, but avoid direct sunlight or it will get as hot as a greenhouse.

THE WATER CYCLE BEGINS!

The plant sucks up water from the soil. The leaves "breathe" out the water, which then evaporates. The air in the jar becomes humid, the water returns to the soil, and the plant starts sucking it up again.

I don't have any clouds or rainstorms in my jar, but sometimes a little water runs down its sides — ALMOST like rain.

water cycle

What do plants need

Do my plants live ONLY on the water I give them? Or do they EAT the soil? I'd better ask Mr. Bloom.

"Plants don't eat the soil itself," says Mr. Bloom. "What they eat are the nutrients in the soil, which are dissolved in water.

"Nitrogen, phosphorus, potassium, iron, and calcium are some of the nutrients that plants need. When your plants suck up the water you give them, they are also absorbing these nutrients."

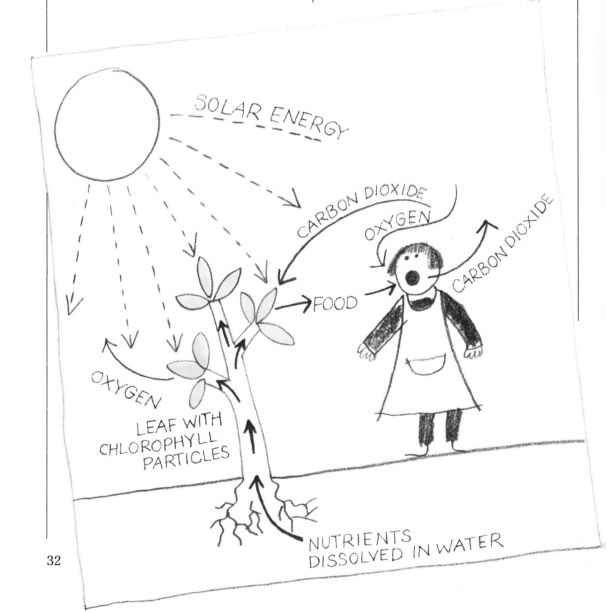

EATING AIR

"There's another thing plants can do," says Mr. Bloom. "They can feed on the AIR."

"Really! How can they do that?"

"It's hard to explain," says Mr. Bloom. "I'll draw you a picture instead.

"Here we have a plant with roots, stem, and flowers. I'll paint the leaves green to show the tiny particles called CHLOROPHYLL.

"The chlorophyll particles in each leaf make the plant's food. It works like this:

"The leaf absorbs CARBON DIOXIDE from the air. The chlorophyll particles use the carbon dioxide to make the plant's nourishment. Mixed with water from the roots, it produces SUGAR, which is the plant's 'food.'

"There is a sort of 'garbage,' too, which is left over after the plant's meal is made. It's the OXYGEN that was in the carbon dioxide. The leaf gets rid of it by releasing it back into the air.

"The sugar that the plant made is later changed into other nutrients that the plant needs to make leaves, branches, flowers, and seeds."

THE SUN
— MOST IMPORTANT OF ALL

"But none of this would ever happen without the SUN," says Mr. Bloom. And he draws a big sun shining down on the leaves with their green chlorophyll particles.

"Chlorophyll is run on solar energy. It needs the sun in order to work."

WITHOUT PLANTS, THERE WOULD BE NO ANIMALS OR PEOPLE

"Aren't there any particles inside me that can make food out of air, water, and sunshine?" I ask.

"No," says Mr. Bloom. "Animals and people don't know how to do it — only plants are that amazing. We also need the sugar and other nutrients that plants make in order to survive, but we get these from plants when we eat them, or when we eat animals that have eaten them.

"Our bodies are able to use this nourishment to grow, move around, think, and do everything else that we do. There are garbage products, too: human waste that we get rid of when we go to the bathroom, and carbon dioxide that we release into the air when we breathe."

"And that the plants can use," I say. "What a perfect system. Everything fits together!"

MORE ABOUT PLANT FOOD (FERTILIZER) ON THE NEXT PAGE ⟶

A WORD ABOUT FERTILIZER

When I buy a bag of potting soil, it usually has all the nutrients that a plant needs.

But after a while, the plant uses up all the nourishment in the soil. Then it's time to give it some new nourishment, or fertilizer, as it is also called.

There are ready-made fertilizers that you can buy in bottles (plant food). I use one of them, mixed with water, when I water my plants.

It's IMPORTANT to follow the directions on the bottle exactly. Plants react badly to an overdose of fertilizer. They can wilt or even die.

And you should NOT fertilize a plant at all when it's blooming or during its dormant (resting) period, which is usually in the winter.

LOOK AT MY GARLIC!

IN THE KITCHEN

you can find lots of things to plant — garlic, for example.

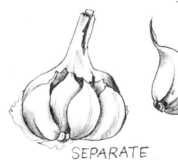

PLANT THE CLOVES POINT UP, ABOUT ONE INCH DEEP (NOT TOO CLOSE)

SEPARATE THE CLOVES

After a couple of weeks, long, narrow leaves poke up. When they are four to five inches long, I start cutting them to use on sandwiches. They're delicious (and milder than garlic).

I cut off the top of a beet and a carrot and planted them each in a pot. I covered them with soil so that just the very top part stuck out.

It wasn't long before small leaves started poking up. And, under the soil, roots were growing.

Now, after only two weeks, I have a little beet "tree" and a carrot "bush."

If I wanted to, I could plant some grass around them and maybe even put some plastic sheep there to graze. We'll see . . .

35

Now I'll teach you the plum game

Today I don't feel like planting anything AT ALL. Some days are like that.

No, today I think I'll go over to Mr. Bloom's and teach him how to play the plum game.

You might as well learn it, too.

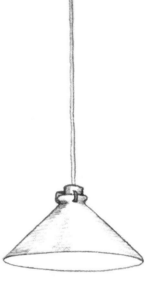

PLUM PITS ←

HERE'S WHAT WE DO:

● I painted eight plum pits with green enamel on one side only. (If you prefer pink, you can use nail polish.)

● Then we put a tablecloth on the table and put forty beans in the center to use for counting points.

● We take turns throwing all the plum pits, keeping track of how many times the green sides come up on top. We use the beans to count points. Here's how we score:.

8 GREEN SIDES UP = 20 POINTS
7 GREEN SIDES UP = 4 POINTS
6 GREEN SIDES UP = 2 POINTS
2 GREEN SIDES UP = 2 POINTS
1 GREEN SIDE UP = 4 POINTS
0 GREEN SIDES UP = 10 POINTS

● Every time you win a point (and take a bean), you get an extra turn. The funny thing is, it almost always comes out four of each, or three and five (which means you don't get any points, of course). Try and explain that!

● When the beans in the pile are all gone, the other players must pay the winner.

● The person who ends up with all the beans wins.

I keep my plum-pit game in a little leather pouch, Indian style. I also have a piece of paper with the rules on it in there — just IN CASE I forget.

MY GAME POUCH

Amaryllis the ugliest

I got an amaryllis bulb for Christmas. It didn't look like much — all brown and dried up. Well, I guess I should plant it anyway, I thought, so I read the directions that came with the bulb:

"Put the lower part of the bulb into a small bowl of water and soak for twenty-four hours," it said. So I did.

Then I planted it in a pot, with a third of the bulb sticking up out of the moist soil. You're not supposed to water it AT ALL for the next eight days (the roots don't want any more water).

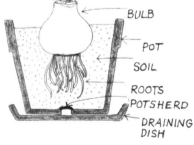

BULB
POT
SOIL
ROOTS
POTSHERD
DRAINING DISH

On the ninth day you water the bulb, but NOT in the POT. Pour lukewarm water into the draining dish. After fifteen minutes, throw away any excess water, and continue to water every other day.

Soon a little green shoot was poking up out of the bulb. It grew higher and higher, and then there were more. They would become the leaves and stems.

After a while, I could see a sort of swelling forming on the top of a stem.

That was the beginning of a bud. One morning, it bloomed! What a surprise — the bud had turned into four flowers! And were they ever BIG! And bright red!

Then one night a loud crack woke me up. The whole pot had fallen — what a CATASTROPHE! The flowers had gotten so heavy that they had tipped over the pot. The thick stem was BROKEN OFF!

It was so sad (I even cried a little). Then I put the broken flower in a glass and set the pot upright again. And that's when I noticed there was ANOTHER stem with a bud on it! I was so happy!

I tied a string around the new stem and fastened it to the wall, so the pot wouldn't tip over again. (Next time, I'll remember to plant an amaryllis in a larger pot!)

There are also white and pink amaryllis. They bloom from September to March.

MY AMARYLLIS STARTED BLOOMING ABOUT FIVE WEEKS AFTER I PLANTED IT

AN AMARYLLIS
IS A LITTLE EXPENSIVE

If you're not lucky enough to get a bulb as a present, maybe you and some friends could buy one together.

1/23   2/2

What is a bulb?

AN AMARYLLIS CAN BLOOM AGAIN!

If you're lucky (and patient), you CAN get an amaryllis to bloom again the next year. Here's what you do:

Remove the whole flower when it dies, but not the leaves.

Mix plant food (fertilizer) into the water you give the bulb, and it will begin to store up nourishment again. (It lost its old nutrients when it produced such enormous flowers!) The leaves help to make the bulb's "food" and will need to have light during this time (see page 33).

Now you'll have to wait all summer for the bulb to grow and recover its strength.

AN AMARYLLIS NEEDS REST

In September, you should stop fertilizing and gradually cut down on the watering as well. The leaves will wilt. Now it's best to put the pot in a cold place (50°F. or so), and not water it at all.

In December, dig up the bulb and throw away the old soil. Plant the amaryllis in a larger pot with fresh soil. And you know what happens next . . .

A NEW FLOWER?

Well no, it's not really a NEW amaryllis that blooms the next year. It's the SAME plant, the same INDIVIDUAL, as Mr. Bloom calls it, that grows back, blooms, and dies, year after year. Amazing!

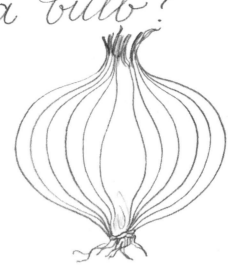

A bulb is really a shoot, wrapped up in thick leaves. The nourishment is stored in the leaves.

Sometimes a bulb divides, producing smaller bulbs. This is called ASEXUAL REPRODUCTION.

In order to have an entirely new INDIVIDUAL, there has to be SEXUAL reproduction. That only happens after FERTILIZATION.

MOM AND DAD

If a plant is going to be fertilized, it has to have both MALE and FEMALE organs.

An amaryllis has both, and most other flowers do too.

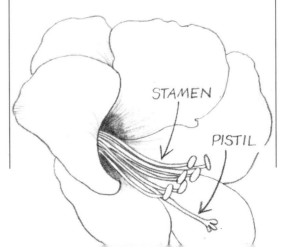

STAMEN

PISTIL

Where do seeds come from?

The female organ is called a PISTIL and the male organ a STAMEN. There is usually ONE pistil and SEVERAL stamen.

On the top of a stamen there are grains of pollen. When one of them sticks to a pistil's stigma, a narrow tube starts growing down into the pistil, to where the egg is stored.

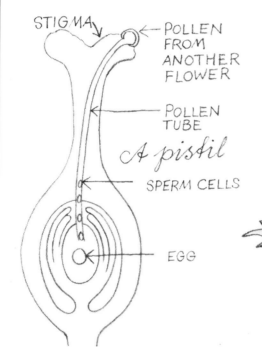

STIGMA

←— POLLEN FROM ANOTHER FLOWER

—— POLLEN TUBE

A pistil

—— SPERM CELLS

—— EGG

Then tiny sperm cells (male sex cells) make their way down the tube to the egg. One of them will penetrate the egg and it will be FERTILIZED.

The fertilized egg will then produce a SEED. When the seed is planted, it will sprout and grow. THAT plant can be said to be a NEW individual, with characteristics from both its mom and its dad.

OH, I ALMOST FORGOT!

Usually pollen from the SAME flower doesn't work. The pistil needs to be pollinated by ANOTHER flower of the same species if anything is going to happen.

BEES

How does pollen get from one flower to another?

Sometimes it just BLOWS over, but usually insects move it from flower to flower — bees, for example.

POLLEN

Flowers attract bees with their sweet-smelling NECTAR. The bees sit on the flowers and suck up the nectar. While they're doing that, some pollen sticks to their "fur." When they fly off to the next flower, some of the pollen falls off.

The bee doesn't know that, of course. He's only interested in the nectar.

INSTEAD OF BEES -SEE PAGE 58

I bought a wooden crate from a store. It had come all the way from China. Just the thing for a mini-garden!

But first I had to waterproof it so it wouldn't leak when I watered the plants.

I bought some heavy-duty plastic (the kind garbage bags are made out of) and lined the crate with it (CAREFULLY, so it wouldn't tear).

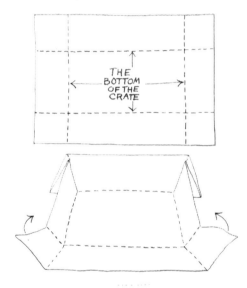

Then I stapled the plastic along the TOP OUTSIDE EDGE (not down inside the crate, or it might leak).

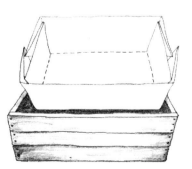

This is how I filled the crate:

The "feather rock" will suck up the excess water, in case I water too much. Since there's no drainage hole in the bottom of the crate, overwatering could cause everything to rot.

A little charcoal mixed in with the feather rock will keep the soil and roots from molding.

A potting mix that includes sand is best for this kind of garden. I had to buy a big bag for mine. (Plant nurseries sell the supplies you will need for your mini-garden.)

I put half of the soil into the crate and watered. Then I poured in the rest and watered again, so it would be moist all the way through.

AN ORDINARY TABLESPOON IS A GOOD PLANTING TOOL

garden!

PALM AND MYRTLE FROM MR. BLOOM

BUSY LIZZIE

PEBBLES

MONKEY MOUNTAIN

MIRROR LAKE

FEATHER ROCK

CHIVE "REEDS"   ORANGE TREE   CACTUS   STONECROP

PLANNING AND PLANTING

Since I wanted to be able to move things around in my garden, I planted some of the plants in their pots. Normally, you would plant them directly in the soil.

It's best if all the plants in your crate have similar watering needs. And don't even bother with fussy plants. I tried one called "baby's tears," which only got sadder and sadder.

I water the chive a little extra (and it likes to be cut often, so it won't droop). The cactus and the stonecrop don't need as much water, since they are desert plants.

Busy Lizzie grew faster than all the others, of course. After a couple of months I had to take her out, so she wouldn't block out the other plants' light.

Almost everyone who raises plants has to deal with bugs sometime. Even Mr. Bloom.

Mr. Bloom says that a plant that has bugs is a dissatisfied plant. There must be something wrong with the water or the room temperature or the light. Or maybe there's a draft. But you can get rid of bugs.

LIZZIE HAS BUGS! HELP!

One day I discovered some tiny bugs crawling around on Lizzie's new leaves and buds. I looked at them through my magnifying glass. Yuck!

I raced to the phone and called Mr. Bloom.

"Help! What should I do? Lizzie is crawling with bugs!"

"Are they light green," he asked, "and very tiny?"

"Yes," I said.

"They must be aphids," he said.

"They're the most common bugs. I'll be right over."

He arrived with some soap and a pair of tweezers.

"Now let's see," he said. "If there hadn't been so many, we could just have picked them off with the tweezers."

"Not me," I said.

"We'll have to try soapy water, instead," said Mr. Bloom.

So we dunked poor Lizzie, pot and all, in a pail of lukewarm soapy water (it has to be

SOAPY WATER

alkali-free soap, not detergent). When we pulled her up again, the aphids were gone. Just to be safe, we took all the plants that had been near Lizzie into the bathroom and gave them a lukewarm shower (without soap).

It was all sticky on the windowsill where Lizzie had been.

"The aphids made that mess, too," said Mr. Bloom.

We had to wash both the window and the sill with soap to clean up after them.

a sad chapter

Last of all, we put Lizzie in a big plastic bag. Mr. Bloom lit a cigarette and blew in some smoke. Quickly we tied the top of the bag and left Lizzie inside for several hours. Poor thing. I'm sure she didn't enjoy it, but it did get rid of the aphids.

Then Mr. Bloom told me about some other pests.

Your Own Bug—

SPIDER MITES

are red-orange and very tiny. They suck the juice from the undersides of leaves, causing the leaves to turn a grayish-yellow color and fall off. If there are many mites, a plant can be covered with webs. They are hard to get rid of without using insecticides. The best way to avoid spider mites is to mist your plants and keep them clean.

THRIPS

are very small insects; they are hard to discover, since the adults fly around. The larvae and pulpae are easier to spot under a plant's leaves. The larvae suck the juice from the leaf, leaving pale-yellow spots. Mist your plants often. Air the room (if it's not too cold), and don't let the plants get too warm.

APHIDS

The most common aphids are light green. They usually cluster on buds or other new plant growth.

Aphids are especially fond of Busy Lizzies.

Treat them with alkali-free soapy water. For another hint, see page 57.

WORMS

live on rotting plant parts, such as roots suffering from overwatering. The worms are completely harmless, and they will disappear if you let the soil dry out between (careful) waterings. If you want to get rid of them even faster, you can put a cigar or cigarette butt on top of the soil. When you water the plant, the poisonous nicotine works its way down into the soil, killing the worms.

SCALE INSECTS

often attack plants that are weak from disease or an overdose of fertilizer. They are harder to get rid of than aphids, since, in their adult stage, they can protect themselves with a little hard oval shell. They feed on plant juices, leaving a light spot on the leaf. The young are hatched out under the shells and then move on to new leaves. If there are enough scale insects, a whole plant can be destroyed.

On thick leaves and stems, you can scrape off the shells. As soon as you discover these pests, wash the plant with soapy water.

WHITEFLIES

are very small, with white wings and bodies that are "powdered" with a white, waxy substance. The adults and the larvae attach themselves to the underside of leaves and feed on the juices. Soapy water doesn't help, since whiteflies simply fly away.

MEALYBUGS

are harder to get rid of. They are a reddish color and are covered with a wax that makes them look as if they have been dipped in flour. The females make small white "cotton balls" to hide their eggs in. Remove the fuzzy balls and brush the mealybugs with alcohol.

WHAT ABOUT INSECTICIDES?

You have probably noticed that plant nurseries and florists sell poisonous insect sprays for killing bugs.

But before you start spraying poison around, try these other methods: spraying with water, alcohol, or a soapy solution; picking off the pests with tweezers or a stick.

IF THAT DOESN'T WORK,

ask at the plant store which insecticide to use, and follow the directions carefully. In the future, check your plants regularly for pests. The earlier you start fighting bugs, the easier it will be to get rid of them before they have multiplied.

Here's a picture that I came across in an old book.

"The Fern Room" — Belgium in the 1850s.

THAT'S how I'd like my room to look! It can't, of course, since I have a perfectly ordinary room. It's not particularly big and has a regular-size window.

But my window does face north, and that's good. East and west windows are okay, too, but plants can get too much sun if they sit in a window facing south.

In the beginning, I kept all my plants on the windowsill, but now I have so many that I've had to find new places for them. Maybe you can get some ideas.

WOODEN CRATES ARE GOOD PLACES

Put plants on top of them in front of the window. They have to be high enough so that the plants will get plenty of light. You can keep plant supplies in the crates.

I KEEP MY GERANIUMS IN A BASKET

so that it's easy to move them when I want to open the window.

for my plants

ON A TABLE BY THE WINDOW

are several crates, but I don't put them too far into the room. All plants need light. The ones farthest away sit on top of another box, so no other plants block out their light.

MY SEED PACKETS

are kept in a little tin that once had tea in it.

I DON'T KNOW

why I put my palm in a glass jar. It just looked like fun.

A CLOTHESLINE

is a good place to hang plant pinups. It's an easy way to show them off (and leave no holes in the wall!).

CLOTHES-LINE

COLD-WEATHER WARNING!

In winter, it can get really cold between the windowpane and the window shade. If you have plants there, don't pull the shade all the way down.

Make sure your windows are weatherproof. Plants don't like drafts.

Move your plants away from the window when airing out a room in the middle of winter. They can freeze (in a minute) and die!

Plants grow out of their pots, just as I grow out of my clothes. Then they need to move into a larger size.

For most plants, the best time for replanting is around the end of February. The winter rest period (dormancy) is over, and they have started growing again. The roots will have a chance to get settled in their new pot.

IS IT TIME?
HERE'S HOW YOU CHECK

First, you water the plant. Then you put the palm of your hand against the soil, hold on to the stem, and turn the pot upside down.

If the soil ball doesn't loosen, tap the pot carefully against a table edge. Pull it out and take a look:

1. Too early for replanting. You can hardly see any roots.

2. Time to replant. You can see lots of roots, and the soil ball doesn't fall apart.

3. Too late! You should have replanted earlier. Poor plant, there's hardly any soil left. (But try, anyway.)

HERE'S HOW TO PLANT

Spread out a newspaper. Get a new and bigger pot, and put a potsherd over the hole.

Remove as much of the old soil as you can WITHOUT harming the roots. Place the plant in the MIDDLE of the new pot (same height as before). Fill the pot with new soil. Press it down, but not TOO hard (about three-quarters of an inch from the top). Water with lukewarm water.

FILL WITH NEW SOIL UP TO HERE

NEW SOIL

POTSHERD

KEEP IT COVERED

You can help your plant by covering it with a plastic bag for the first few days. The bag must have air holes.

If you don't use a bag, you should at least spray the leaves with water. It's important for the plant not to dry out. But don't water too much, either, or the roots won't be able to breathe.

WHICH POT SHOULD I USE?

There are clay pots and plastic pots. Mr. Bloom says he doesn't know which are better, but here are some things to know about both:

CLAY POTS let the air get through to the roots, but the soil dries out faster.

PLASTIC POTS are light and cheap, but they are airtight. The soil doesn't dry out as easily, so you should water them less.

Most of my pots are clay, because I think they're prettier. If you have clay pots, too, remember:

1. New pots must soak for at least twenty-four hours before you plant anything in them. Otherwise, they can steal the plant's water.

2. If you plant something in a used pot, make sure it is CLEAN. Scrub it, inside and out, with a brush, using hot, soapy water.

3. Do NOT paint a pot. That would make it airtight.

POTSHERDS

Always put one or more potsherds (bits of broken pottery) over the drainage hole. That way, excess water (but not soil or roots) can drain out.

I lined a plastic lid with wet cotton and sowed some garden-cress seeds on it.

Then I put my little cress garden on the windowsill and made sure that the cotton stayed moist.

The garden-cress seeds sprouted quickly, and after a week I had quite a crop.

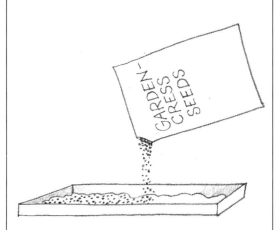

Soon it was time to harvest, so I carefully cut off all the green leaves.

P.S. LOW SIDES - OTHERWISE, IT WOULD BE HARD TO CUT

52

And now I'll tell you what you can do with garden-cress:

GARDEN-CRESS EGGS

Hard-boil some eggs for ten minutes. Rinse them in cold water. Peel and cut them in two, lengthwise.

Carefully scoop out the yolks and put them in a bowl. Add some mayonnaise or cream and mix well. Season with salt and pepper and lots of garden cress.

Fill the egg whites with the mixture. Yum!

easy and delicious!

GARDEN-CRESS CHEESE

Pour one cup of sour cream into a coffee filter. Let it drain over a cup for twenty-four hours.

When the time is up, you will see that about a third of a cup of liquid (whey) has filtered into the cup. The sour cream in the filter has thickened. It has turned into cheese.

Season it with salt, pepper, and lots of chopped garden cress. You might want to try adding other herbs: Italian seasoning, for example.

YOU CAN USE.
YOGURT TOO,
BUT I THINK
SOUR CREAM TASTES BEST

MR. BLOOM
LIKES
GARLIC,
WHICH
REMINDS
ME . . .

What a great idea! I'll give Mr. Bloom a crock of garden-cress cheese for his birthday! But first I'll squeeze a clove of fresh garlic (better than powder) into his cheese. Then I'll tie a piece of cloth over the top to make it look nice.

LINNEA'S GARDEN-CRESS CHEESE

Happy

I COLORED HALF THE ROSE GREEN!

WATER WITH FOOD COLORING

WATER WITHOUT FOOD COLORING

birthday, Mr Bloom!

Mr. Bloom is getting another present from me, too — a rose that is half white and half green. It's TRUE! It really works. I cut the stem of a white rose down the middle, and put one half in a glass with clear water and the other half in a glass with water and green food coloring.

A few hours later, exactly half the rose had turned green. That's not as odd as it seems. A rose sucks up water through tiny tubes in its stem. Half the stem sucked up clear water, and the other half, colored water.

(It works just as well with other flowers and other colors.)

"Happy birthday, Mr. Bloom!"

The Green 🌿 Gazette

How to fool seeds

Some pits can't start to grow (germinate) without a period of winterrest (dormancy).

That's how it is with cherries, plums, pears, apples, and hazelnuts.

But you can fool a pit into BELIEVING that winter is over. Here's how:

Cover the pit with sand and keep it in the refrigerator (not the freezer) for three months. Then plant it the usual way.

Pits with thick shells
can be rubbed with sandpaper before planting. That makes it easier for water to get through the shell, and they will germinate faster. Try it with apricot, peach, olive, and walnut pits.

Date pits are real lazy-bones
It can take FOREVER for them to germinate. I know someone who had to wait more than a year! Try putting some date pits in an open glass jar lined with wet cotton. Keep the jar in a warm place, and don't let the cotton dry out.

Extra light from a light bulb

If you suspect that your plants are getting too little light, you can give them an extra dose. You can use an ordinary light bulb, but it's better to buy a special daylight plant light. They are sold in plant-supply stores. Unfortunately, they are more expensive than ordinary light bulbs.

Don't throw it away!

Poinsettias are popular Christmas presents. They have both red and green leaves and are beautiful, until they lose all their leaves. The red ones fall off first, then the green. Most people throw the plant away at that point.

But not me. I saved my poinsettia and cut it down to almost nothing.

By April, it was already showing signs of new life. Green leaves appeared, but no red leaves or flowers.

You CAN get it to bloom. Look it up in a plant-care manual to find out how.

The Green 🍃 Gazette

Lizzie can start from seed, too

I bought some Busy Lizzie seeds and planted them. The cutest little Lizzies came up, and they did just as well as my old Lizzie (page 20).

(You can plant geranium seeds, too, and get really nice flowers.)

I planted lots of Lizzies in small flowerpots. They make great presents!

Ladybugs are useful insects. They eat aphids and scale insects. Take a few home to your plants if they have bugs. (But don't use insecticides after that, or the ladybugs will die, too.)

IT ISN'T TRUE,

as some people say, that you have to STEAL a cutting in order for it to grow. It's always better to ask permission first.

Save an artichoke

Put it in a window and let it bloom. It will be beautiful.

A white coating

on your clay pots is normal — don't worry about it.

Pebbles in the draining dish

allow a plant to keep its "feet" above water. Gravel works, too.

The Green 🍃 Gazette

In an old book

I found this picture from 1850. Here's proof that the idea of making a little water cycle in a glass jar (page 30) is not new. But I feel sorry for the little animals trapped in this one.

PIGGYBACK PLANT

I saw a really pretty plant that I'm going to buy next spring. It's called a piggyback plant because it has little leaves growing "piggyback" on top of bigger leaves.

How long can you save a seed?

It depends on the type of seed, but it's always best to plant seeds the same year you buy them. (Garden-cress can be saved a couple of years.) Seeds stored in air-tight containers last longer. That explains why seeds that were buried in dry sand or hidden under peat bogs are able to germinate after hundreds of years.

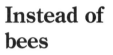

Instead of bees

When you want a flower to be pollinated and there aren't any bees around (indoors, for example), you can do the job yourself. You can "pollinate" from one flower to another with a paintbrush!

An experiment:

NO GREEN WITHOUT SUNLIGHT

I found a potato that had started to sprout in a dark pantry. The sprouts were white.

When I took the potato out into the light, the sprouts soon turned green.

What's the problem?

In the left column is a list of problems plants can have. Follow the line out to the right until you come to a green X. The category above the X gives a possible cause for the problem. There are often several reasons.

CAUSE → / PROBLEM ↓	Too much water	Too little water	Air too dry	Too dark	Too sunny	Too cold	Drafty	Too little fertilizer	Too much fertilizer	Needs replanting	Needs pruning	Bugs
Drops leaves		X	X	X			X					X
Droops	X	X			X			X	X			
Yellows	X	X		X	X		X		X			
Small, pale leaves				X		X		X		X		X
Grows poorly							X	X	X	X		
Leaf edges dry out		X	X									
Doesn't bloom				X				X	X			
Tall and skinny				X							X	
Pale spots					X							X
Holes in the leaves												X
White "cotton balls," "spiderwebs"												X
Sticky stuff on the windowsill												X

THERE ARE OTHER PROBLEMS ...

BUT THESE WERE THE ONES WE CAME UP WITH HAVE FUN!